CW01082933

Original title:
Better Days

Editor: Jessica Elisabeth Luik
Author: Liina Liblikas
ISBN HARDBACK: 978-9916-86-062-5
ISBN PAPERBACK: 978-9916-86-063-2

Radiant Tomorrows

In the heart of night
New dreams gently form
Guided by starlight
Through the midnight storm

Whispers of fate
In twilight's embrace
Agendas they state
With delicate grace

Beyond the sorrow
A horizon gleams
Of radiant morrow
Full of daring dreams

Echoes of Dawn

When night's curtain falls
Dawn's whispers arise
Awakening calls
From slumbering skies

First light softly glows
Kissing the dews
Breathing life, it knows
Worlds to bemuse

Nature in chorus
Sings morning's song
A serene force
Where hearts belong

Infinite Horizons

Beyond the skyline
Infinite hues blend
Horizons entwine
Stories never end

Miles stretch afar
Adventures await
Glimmered by stars
Dictated by fate

Journeys unknown
Promises unfound
Vast lands overgrown
Wonders unbound

Blooming Futures

Beneath the old trees
Seeds of hope sowed
Whispering the breeze
Where dreams often rode

In fields softly spun
With threads of delight
New futures begun
Embrace morning's light

Petals unfold
Of futures in bloom
Tender tales told
Dispelling the gloom

Glimmers of Dawn

Silent whispers greet the morn,
Colors tenderly are born.
Skies of blue and pink adorn,
Nature's symphony is sworn.

Stars retreat as daylight grows,
Morning's breath in sweet repose.
Softly, through the fields it flows,
Where each petal gently shows.

Serendipity Sunrise

Radiance breaks the night's embrace,
Warmth spreads through the silent space.
Chance encounters set the pace,
Morning's gift, a gentle grace.

Birds awake with songs anew,
Dew-kissed flowers bloom in view.
Serendipity shines through,
Day begins with skies of blue.

Mornings Unbound

Crisp and clear the dawn unfolds,
Promises the light beholds.
Stories of the day are told,
In the hues of morning gold.

Boundless dreams in sunlight stream,
Awaking from the land of dreams.
Life anew in morning's gleam,
Ever bright, as it redeems.

Embracing Sunrise

Awakened hearts to morning's glow,
With every beam, the spirits grow.
In dawn's embrace, we come to know,
The endless paths where we may go.

Golden light on fields of green,
Whispers of what might have been.
Pastel skies, a tranquil scene,
Breathing in the day's serene.

Ray's Promise

In morning light where shadows play,
The dawn arrives, a dance of day.
Whispers of dreams in golden hue,
Begin anew with skies so blue.

A promise held in every beam,
Chases away the darkest dream.
In every ray, a hope anew,
For hearts to mend and spirits, true.

The world awakes with gentle grace,
Sun's warm embrace on every face.
In Ray's promise, love does grow,
For in its light, all truth shall show.

Endless Dawn

An endless dawn, horizon's kiss,
A timeless grace, embrace of bliss.
In every breath, a whisper clear,
Of hope and dreams, forever near.

The stars retreat, night's gentle sway,
As colors bloom in light of day.
A symphony of light and sound,
In endless dawn, our hearts unbound.

New chapters start, the past is gone,
With endless dawn, life marches on.
Embrace the day, let worries cease,
In endless dawn, we find our peace.

Sunrise Symphony

A symphony begins at dawn,
Where night recedes and day is drawn.
The notes of morning, crisp and clear,
Awaken life, erase all fear.

Birdsongs echo, sky's crescendo,
Colors paint a grand allegro.
In this orchestra of light,
The world rejoices in warm delight.

Each sunrise brings a melody,
Of hope and sweet tranquility.
In sunrise symphony we find,
Harmony of heart and mind.

Reaching Dawn

Through sleepless night and starry skies,
We journey forth as dark complies.
Awaiting light, our spirits drawn,
To touch the edge of reaching dawn.

Each step we take, a closer stride,
To where the sun and dreams collide.
Embrace the glow, unfurl your wings,
As dawn arrives and softly sings.

In reaching dawn, our hopes align,
A brand new day, a chance to shine.
Embrace the light, let shadows fade,
For in this dawn, new paths are laid.

Uplifted Skies

In the dawn's early embrace,
Sunrise paints with golden grace,
Clouds part with gentle eyes,
Welcome to the uplifted skies.

Winds whisper dreams untold,
Horizons in their fold,
Hearts soar where freedom lies,
Beyond these uplifted skies.

Stars still whisper last goodbyes,
As night softly dies,
New hopes begin to rise,
Beneath uplifted skies.

Untarnished Dreams

In the quiet of the night,
Where stars hold dreams tight,
Whispers of what could be,
In a world endlessly free.

Paths of silver moonbeams,
Guide our untarnished dreams,
Promising the unseen,
In the waking gleam.

Hope's light softly streams,
Into our untarnished dreams,
Lighting futures bright,
In the deepest night.

Blossoming Future

In the garden of tomorrow,
Seeds escape their sorrow,
With each blooming hour,
Comes a blossoming flower.

Roots strengthen, tall they rise,
Beneath the vast blue skies,
New beginnings ever pure,
Mark a blossoming future.

Petals catch the morning dew,
As old dreams start anew,
In hope we find our cure,
For a blossoming future.

Comforting Light

In shadows deep and wide,
Where fears often hide,
Comes a soothing sight,
A comforting light.

Guiding through the dark,
Igniting hope's sweet spark,
Embracing every heart tight,
With comforting light.

As the night gives way,
To the dawn of a new day,
We'll bask in the warm delight,
Of a comforting light.

Luminescent Tomorrows

Beyond the haze, where futures gleam,
A path is drawn by moon's bright beam.
In shadows cast by stars so bright,
We dream of journeys through the night.

Through valleys deep, where echoes ring,
Our hearts take flight and spirits sing.
Horizons whisper untold tales,
Of luminescent, vibrant trails.

Embrace the glow that morning sends,
A dawn where fear and darkness ends.
In woven threads of hope and grace,
We find our place in time and space.

Dreams Set Free

In the garden of whispered dreams,
Where wishes glide on moonlit streams.
A world unfolds, unseen by day,
Where shadows dance and hopes don't stray.

Each star a guide, each breeze a muse,
Imaginations gently fuse.
With every sigh, the night bestows,
A symphony where freedom flows.

Awakened minds, unchained, unbound,
On silvered wings, our souls are found.
In twilight's realm, we cease to be,
Mere echoes—now, we're dreams set free.

Sunbeam Serenade

When morning's light begins to play,
And chases sleep's last ghost away.
The sun's soft kiss on velvet skies,
Awakens earth with gentle sighs.

Through dewdrop fields where lilies bloom,
A chorus hums, dispelling gloom.
Each petal glows with golden hue,
In sunbeam's song so pure and true.

With nature's grace in radiant stream,
We waltz within a waking dream.
A melody of warmth and light,
In sunbeam serenade so bright.

Embrace the Dawn

As night's embrace begins to fade,
We greet the dawn in hope arrayed.
With every ray, a promise new,
The world awakens, touched by dew.

Mountains bathed in morning's gold,
Whispered tales of days unfold.
In skies brushed blue, horizons wide,
We cast off fears and let dreams ride.

Each heartbeat sings with morning's grace,
In sunrise colors we find place.
With dawn's embrace, we boldly stride,
Into the world, with hearts open wide.

Hearts Renewed

In the dawn of whispered dreams,
Hearts ignite in soft sunrise beams.
From the past, we've gently sewn,
Love renewed, as seeds are sown.

Echoes fade in morning's light,
Hope emerges, day and night.
Beneath the sky, our souls aligned,
Bound by bonds, so intertwined.

Silent vows beneath the stars,
Hearts that heal and shed their scars.
Each new breath, a chance to fly,
In love's arms, we'll always lie.

Tranquil Tomorrows

Silver waves on crystal sand,
Blissful peace we understand.
In the quiet, find our way,
To a new and gentle day.

Whispers ride on evening's breeze,
Calmness found within the trees.
Eyes that gaze on boundless skies,
Tranquil tomorrows, no goodbyes.

Softly tread on paths untold,
Jewels of serenity, we'll hold.
As the night fades into dawn,
Every fear and worry gone.

Vision Beyond

Stars align with dreams in sight,
Guiding hearts through endless night.
Visions of a world so clear,
Whispers cast away our fear.

In the stillness, futures gleam,
Boundless hope, a vivid dream.
Eyes look past the veils of today,
Seeker's soul will find the way.

Through the mist, where shadows fall,
We will rise and stand tall.
A vision crafted by our hand,
In new horizons, we will stand.

Shattered Shadows

Whispers in the midnight gloom,
Like flowers lost before they bloom.
Shattered shadows on the floor,
Fragments of what was before.

In the silence, grief does mend,
Wounds that time and love can tend.
From the darkness, light will grow,
A phoenix rising from the woe.

Broken pieces come to form,
Something new from the storm.
In the dawn of gentle hues,
Shattered shadows, now renewed.

Dreams Awakened

In slumber's gentle embrace
Visions softly take flight
Whispers of hope cascade
Through the quiet of night

Stars twinkle their secrets
Upon a silken sky
Beyond horizon's edge
Ideas begin to fly

Mystic realms explored
With hearts unguardedly
The infinite unfolds
Dreams of eternity

Eyes flutter, pulse quickens
Horizons kiss the dawn
Awakened from the veil
A new world is drawn

The past shadows quiver
Future paths illuminate
Dreams give voice to the night
In moments of create

Boundless Light

Beneath the boundless sky
Where endless reaches go
A whispering breeze arises
In a golden, gentle show

Horizons melt in color
As the day turns to flame
Spirits rise with twilight
None the same, none the same

Torches in the dark ignite
Souls once lost now gleam
In the tapestry of stars
Light weaves through the seam

Night's canvas paints desires
With a cosmic, radiant hand
Boundless dreams ignite the stars
In a cosmic, muse-led band

Wisdom whispers softly
In the quiet of the night
Eternal echoes resonate
In realms of boundless light

Promise of Morning

The world in silence waits
For dawn's first tender kiss
A palette of soft hues
Promise a morning's bliss

Birds with songs awaken
The rhythm of the day
Echoes of magic linger
As night whispers away

Mists rise from hidden glades
In dances pure and slow
Nature hums a hymn
To land where dreams grow

Fragrant winds caress
Fields touched by hopeful rays
In the arms of morning
Love's eternal praise

New horizons shimmer
Promises brightly drawn
Within the heart of dawn
A world, reborn

Emerging Radiance

In the hush of twilight
Where day meets night
A glow emerges softly
With a gentle light

Stars begin their vigil
Guardians of the sky
In the quiet moments
Energies amplify

Hope rises like a phoenix
With wings of golden grace
A symphony of colors
Spreads through time and space

Dreams align with stardust
In a dance of fate
Emerging radiance unfolds
Transcending gate

Through the dark and daylight
In every heart and hand
A brilliant light emerges
Across life's wide expanse

Sunrise of Hope

In the cradle of morning light,
Dreams awaken, taking flight.
Golden hues of dawn arise,
Chasing darkness from the skies.

Whispers soft of a new day,
Banish fears, keep doubts at bay.
Every shadow fades away,
Hope's embrace is here to stay.

Mountains glow in amber hues,
Winds of change, a gentle muse.
Birds sing songs of fresh renew,
Sunrise paints the world anew.

Whispers of Tomorrow

In the silence of the night,
Dreams are woven with pure light.
Echoes of the future near,
Sending whispers we can hear.

Stars are guides that softly gleam,
On the path to every dream.
In their glow, the road is clear,
Steps of faith, we hold dear.

Promises in twilight's grace,
Lay the fears we must erase.
Whispers of tomorrow's face,
Brings us to a brighter space.

A New Dawn

When the veil of night does fade,
Morning brings a fresh parade.
Colors rise with grand display,
Heralding a brand new day.

Worries melt in soft sunlight,
Birthing hope with each first sight.
Through the mist, the path is drawn,
Guided by the early dawn.

Mountains stand in calm repose,
Nature's hymn in subtle prose.
Soft and bright, the day unfolds,
In new dawn, life gently holds.

Echoes of Promise

In the breeze of twilight's air,
Lies a promise, pure and fair.
Dreams conceived in light's embrace,
Find their form in gentle grace.

Stars will whisper tales anew,
Of the hopes we'll journey to.
Promise rolls like ocean's tide,
Steady, constant, by our side.

Paths of light shall guide us on,
To the realms of dusk and dawn.
Echoes in the heart will stay,
Carrying us on our way.

Skyward Dreams

Beneath the stars, our visions gleam,
On silver wings, we chase the theme,
Of countless nights, our souls afire,
Ascending higher, hearts aspire.

Through clouds of white, through skies azure,
We journey forth with spirits pure,
Where starlit paths and moonbeams guide,
In endless dreams, with cosmic pride.

A universe so vast, unknown,
With secrets whispered, softly sown,
In twilight's glow, our hopes declare,
Skyward dreams, beyond compare.

Glory Days Ahead

In morning's light, our hopes arise,
With eyes aglow, we greet the skies,
For every dawn, a promise true,
Of glory days, in shades of blue.

The paths ahead, although unknown,
We stride with strength, as seeds are sown,
With courage fierce, and hearts so bright,
We conquer fear, embrace the light.

Beyond the hills, past trials long,
We'll march with faith, our spirits strong,
For in our hearts, the future spread,
A tapestry, by glory led.

Blossom of Hope

In fields where shadows once were cast,
A single bloom has grown so fast,
Its petals bright, with dewdrops sprayed,
A blossom of hope, undeterred, unafraid.

From barren ground, its roots extend,
Against the odds, it will ascend,
With every sunbeam, every rain,
Hope blossoms forth through joy and pain.

Amid the trials, amid the strife,
Its colors vivid, bringing life,
A symbol pure, for hearts to cope,
In every flower, a bloom of hope.

New Light

When darkness fades, new light appears,
Dispelling shadows, calming fears,
A dawn of golden warmth and grace,
Illuminates the landscape's face.

The night departs, a silent flight,
With morning's touch, the world alight,
The whispers of a hopeful start,
New light that shines upon the heart.

Through mists that fade with morning's breath,
A fresh beginning conquers death,
With every ray, our spirits bright,
Embrace the day, with new-found light.

Fields of Possibility

In fields where dreams align
With whispers of the breeze
Our hopes like stars will shine
Amidst the endless seas

The earth beneath our feet
Holds secrets yet untold
With courage, we shall meet
New worlds, as they unfold

In every budding leaf
A story comes to light
Life conquers pain and grief
In dawn's embrace, so bright

Possibilities unbound
Take flight on wings of hope
In vast expanse, profound
We find the strength to cope

With every step we take
The future's path reveals
In dreams, we'll never break
In fields where truth appeals

Soul's Rebirth

In twilight's tender grasp
The soul begins its song
Through shadows, fingers clasp
To where we all belong

A whisper in the night
Awakens dreams anew
With dawn's first golden light
The heart finds courage, too

From ashes, we shall rise
A phoenix in the sky
With fierce, determined eyes
To touch the heavens high

Every tear and sorrow
Becomes the forge's flame
A brighter, bold tomorrow
Emerges from the same

The spirit, vast and free
In every breath, restored
The soul's rebirth to see
Our essence, now adored

Courageous Mornings

In mornings bright and clear
With courage born of night
The dawn dispels our fear
And fills our hearts with light

Each sunrise brings resolve
To face the day's demands
Our spirits will evolve
As strength fills weary hands

The morning mist retreats
Before the breaking sun
In every heart, it beats
A new day's race begun

Through trials we will tread
With fortitude and grace
A future lies ahead
We cross with steady pace

As morning's hues unfold
Our purpose comes to view
Each breath, a story told
In skies of endless blue

Symphony of Light

A symphony of light
Unfolds with each new ray
The stars that grace the night
Now yield to break of day

In every golden strand
The music softly plays
As light takes nature's hand
In delicate displays

The world begins to hum
In harmony so sweet
A melody begun
In sunbeams at our feet

Through colors pure and bright
They paint the morning sky
In symphony of light
Our spirits learn to fly

The beauty all around
Composed in nature's art
In every sight and sound
A symphony, our heart

Whispers of Renewal

In shadows deep, where dreams entwine,
Lost moments find their tender grace,
Leaves murmur secrets with the pine,
Whispers of renewal trace.

Through twilight's veil, the stars align,
A symphony of night's embrace,
Renew the spirit, soul's design,
In nature's calm, we find our place.

Beneath the moon's soft, silver shine,
The world becomes a sacred space,
Where hearts can heal and hopes refine,
With whispers light as silk and lace.

Morning Glories

The dawn unfolds in hues so bright,
Morning glories greet the sun,
Embracing day with pure delight,
A new beginning has begun.

Each petal whispers soft and light,
A song of life in every one,
In calm and joy, dispelling night,
Morning glories weave and spun.

With dewdrop crowns in morning's light,
They spark a dance, a graceful run.
Nature's promise held in sight,
Morning glories, day's first fun.

Awakening Hearts

In silence, hearts begin to wake,
To whispers soft, the dawn's first kiss,
A gentle breeze, a lover's ache,
In morning's glow, we find our bliss.

The stillness breaks with life's sweet song,
Awakening hearts in tender sway,
To new beginnings we belong,
Each breath a promise, every day.

In love's embrace, forever strong,
Our souls in harmony will stay,
Awakening hearts where we belong,
In timeless dance, come what may.

Eternal Springs

Eternal springs where waters flow,
In timeless currents kind and clear,
Where blossoms bloom as breezes blow,
A symphony for heart and ear.

Beneath the azure, skies bestow,
A gift of life, a pledge sincere,
In this place where dreams can grow,
Love's eternal whisper near.

With each new dawn, the springs will show,
A world reborn, an endless year,
Through seasons' dance, the heart will know,
Eternal springs, forever dear.

Endless Sunrises

Each dawn, the sky alights with grace,
Hues of gold and crimson blend.
A promise born in night's embrace,
Awakens hope, where dreams ascend.

Waves of light on morning's crest,
Touch the earth with tender sighs.
Nature stirs from peaceful rest,
Beneath the endless, painted skies.

Whispers of the night depart,
As the sun begins to rise.
A new day blooms within the heart,
In the glow of morning's prize.

From Darkness to Dawn

Nighttime's cloak, so vast and deep,
Covers lands in silent sweep.
Dreams arise from slumbered keep,
Promising the dawn to peep.

Stars dissolve as light intrudes,
Shadows fade where morning broods.
Hope renews in brightened moods,
Life reborn in dawn's preludes.

From the dark, the light extends,
Casting warmth, where twilight bends.
Day unfolds as night rescinds,
A fresh start, life's true amends.

Promise of Light

Through the night, the promise gleams,
A distant glow in darkened streams.
Silent stars and moonlit beams,
Herald light in whispered dreams.

Morning's touch dispels the night,
Chasing shadows out of sight.
Every dawn renews the fight,
For a world bathed in light.

Paths once cloaked in shades of grey,
Now reveal the breaking day.
In the light, we find our way,
Promises of hope relay.

Radiant Mornings

Morning light breaks, the day begins
Golden rays on gentle winds
Nature stirs with tender grace
Whispers of the dawn's embrace

Birds awaken, songs they share
Spreading music to the air
Petals open, fresh and bright
Greeting the early morning light

Soft breezes through the trees they glide
Calm and peaceful, far and wide
Stars retreat, their glow subdued
Embracing daylight's interlude

Meadows stretching far and green
Sparkling with a dewy sheen
Each new dawn, a promise born
In the heart of radiant morn

Echoes carry, time to rise
Light reflecting in our eyes
New horizons to explore
Radiant mornings forevermore

Silent Triumphs

In quiet moments, strength is found
A whispered joy, a soft resound
Not all wins are loud and bright
Triumphs live in silent light

Through the storms, we stand so firm
Quiet hearts, resolve confirmed
Every challenge, every stride
Silent victories reside

In the night, when darkness creeps
Courage in the silence seeps
Through the shadows shines a gleam
Of resilience, like a dream

The silent cheer, the gentle praise
Lifting spirits through the haze
Strength in silence, quiet might
Guiding us to morning's light

Silent triumphs, softly held
In each heart, a story spelled
Unseen glory, strength anew
Silent triumphs carry through

Sapphire Horizons

Above the ocean, skies so blue
Whisper dreams anew, and true
Waves embrace the endless shore
Sapphire horizons to explore

The sun descends, a fiery blaze
Reflected in the ocean's glaze
As day fades to twilight's hue
Sapphire tones in every view

Moonlight dances on the sea
A tranquil, shimmering jubilee
Stars appear, their silver light
Guiding sailors through the night

Boundless sky and deep blue waves
Mark the paths that courage paves
On horizons, bold and wide
Adventure shimmers, ebbing tide

Sapphire dreams, horizon's call
In their depths, we lose it all
Venturing to distant lands
With tomorrow in our hands

Awakening Joy

Joy awakens with the dawn
Spreading like a sleepy yawn
Hearts arise, their spirits bright
Bathed in morning's golden light

Moments precious, smiles unfold
Feelings warm and stories told
Happiness in every sigh
As the day begins to fly

Fields of laughter, skies of cheer
Every moment, held so dear
Joyful echoes fill the air
Spreading goodness everywhere

Each new day, a gift to hold
Joyful moments, soft yet bold
Hearts awaken once again
In a world where joy sustains

Awakening joy, bright and free
A symphony of unity
Coming forth with morning dew
In every heart, a joy anew

Future Blossoms

In time's garden, seeds we sow,
Dreams that dance in evening's glow,
Moments fleeting, yet they stay,
Whispers of a coming day.

Beneath the soil, life does stir,
Roots of hope begin to purr,
Petals reach with all their might,
Seeking warmth in day's first light.

Softly blooms the future's call,
Past and present in its thrall,
Colors blend in vibrant hues,
Promises of morning's views.

Nature's canvas, ever sweet,
Paths unknown beneath our feet,
Journey forward, heart in hand,
In this world of future's land.

Fragile buds, with strength do rise,
To embrace wide-open skies,
Eternal cycles, round they spin,
In tomorrow's blooms, we begin.

Golden Horizons

Morning breaks with gilded light,
Chasing shadows from the night,
Sky ablaze with hues anew,
Promises of dreams in view.

Mountains tall, horizon grand,
Secrets held within their hand,
Golden beams on distant crest,
Whispers of a quest unblessed.

Valleys echo morning's tune,
Sunrise bathed in glow of noon,
Through the vast expanse we roam,
Seeking worlds we call our own.

Twilight nears, yet hope remains,
In the light that softly wanes,
Golden moments, fleeting fast,
Echoes of a future vast.

Horizons wide, we chase the dawn,
In its gleaming, we are drawn,
Journey ends where it began,
In the heart of every man.

Threads of Light

In the fabric of the night,
Woven lines of purest light,
Glimmers dance with silken grace,
Lending warmth to empty space.

Stars as jewels, they softly gleam,
Guardians of every dream,
Threads of silver, threads of gold,
Stories through the ages told.

Heaven's tapestry unfolds,
Mysteries that time withholds,
Binding hearts across the skies,
In their gleaming, we arise.

Echoes in the twilight's span,
Linking every child to man,
Threads of light, forever spun,
Weaving into one by one.

Night's embrace, and still they guide,
Lights unseen, yet never hide,
Through the dark and through the bright,
We are bound in threads of light.

Rise Above Shadows

From the depths where darkness lies,
Hope, like dawn, begins to rise,
Shadows cast their fleeting forms,
Amid life's relentless storms.

Heartbeats echo, bold and true,
Through the trials, we renew,
Silent whispers, rising loud,
Bursting through each doubt's dark shroud.

Sunlight pierces, breaks the night,
Gifts us with its gentle might,
Rise above, with wings of grace,
Find our place in endless space.

Every trial's a passing phase,
Light remains in darkest days,
Rise, we shall, with spirits strong,
To the world, our hopeful song.

Shadows part, the path is clear,
Courage overcomes each fear,
Rise above, with hearts that soar,
In the light, forevermore.

Spun Gold Mornings

In the hush of dawn's soft gleaming,
Golden threads of light unfold,
Whispers of the day start streaming,
As night's tales are gently told.

Fields and valleys bathed in wonder,
Wake beneath the golden hue,
Birds take flight as soft as thunder,
Sky painted in shades anew.

Dreams dissolve in morning's splendor,
Daybreak kisses slumber's cheek,
Moments fragile, sweetly tender,
Mysteries the sun will seek.

Echoes of the night retreating,
Warmth spreads across the land,
Heartbeats in the morning greeting,
Hourglass of time in hand.

Fields of gold in morning's treasure,
Every ray a promise sworn,
Life begins, a perfect measure,
In the spun gold of the morn.

Transcending Twilight

Shadows dance in twilight's linger,
Whispers weave through evening's grace,
Stars are painted with a finger,
Night descends in soft embrace.

Hues of violet, deepest crimson,
Blend where day and night converge,
Mystic realms in light's redaction,
We, through stardust, gently surge.

Voices of the past grow clearer,
Echoes from a time untold,
Twilight's veil brings them nearer,
Fables of the stars unfold.

Dreams take flight in timeless fashion,
Boundless skies in twilight blue,
Love and hope, in silent passion,
Fill the void as darkness grew.

In the twilight, trust the leisure,
Beauty in the world alight,
Moments held, a precious treasure,
Transcending day into the night.

First Light

Crimson kissed with hints of amber,
First light's breath upon the earth,
Dewdrops shimmer, soft and tender,
Day awakes, a wondrous birth.

Birdsong greets the hopeful breaking,
Whispers of the night recede,
In the glow, our dreams are waking,
Heartbeats fast with every need.

Silent night's embrace is fading,
Colors burst in morning's hue,
Every heart, the light invading,
Drawing strength to start anew.

Morning's touch, a healer's blessing,
Banishing the dark of night,
In this dawn, the world confessing,
Truths revealed in perfect light.

First light calls with gentle power,
Promising the coming day,
Life begins, a fragrant flower,
In the dawn's first tender ray.

Boundless Mornings

Early light drapes the earth in ease,
Gentle winds whisper through the trees.
A symphony of birds takes flight,
Heralding the promise of the night.

Dew-kissed petals greet the sun,
The day's adventures just begun.
Boundless mornings stretch ahead,
Painting skies in hues of red.

Golden beams caress the land,
Waves of warmth on the sand.
Dreams awaken with each ray,
Chasing shadows far away.

Golden Tomorrows

Beneath the heavens vast and grand,
We tread on life's uncharted sand.
Dreams unfurl with every dawn,
Golden tomorrows, hope reborn.

Stars that fade with morning's light,
Pass the torch to skies so bright.
In each heart a fire ignites,
Guiding us through endless nights.

Paths unknown, but steps are true,
Towards horizons painted blue.
In the dance of days to come,
Golden tomorrows, here we run.

Whispers of Dawn

As night surrenders, shadows fall,
First light breaks through, a gentle call.
Whispers of dawn fill the air,
A tender promise everywhere.

The quiet hum of morning's breath,
Banishes the night's sweet death.
Awakening the world anew,
With colors bathed in morning dew.

Silent moments, softly kissed,
By the early morning mist.
Whispers of dawn, a quiet song,
Welcoming the day so strong.

Seeds of Joy

In fields of green with skies so clear,
We plant the seeds of joy and cheer.
Each smile a bloom, each laugh a flower,
Growing tall with every hour.

Underneath the sun's embrace,
Simple moments, love's true grace.
In the garden of our days,
Joyful seeds sprout through the haze.

With gentle hands we sow the light,
Turning darkness into bright.
From seeds of joy, life is spun,
Harvesting happiness, one by one.

Golden Horizons

As dawn breaks forth in golden hue,
The world awakens, fresh and new.
Mountains kiss the sky so vast,
Echoes of dreams from ages past.

Morning light on fields of green,
Reflects upon the tranquil scene.
Birdsongs weave a melody bright,
Welcoming the day's first light.

Waves caress the sandy shore,
Whispers of tales from times of yore.
With each crest, the past unfurls,
Embracing sailors, seeking pearls.

Golden horizons stretch afar,
Guiding ships by light of star.
Hope afloat on oceans wide,
In boundless seas, dreams reside.

As sunset descends, soft and slow,
Shadows lengthen, moonlights glow.
Night provides a gentle balm,
Under stars, the world is calm.

New Beginnings

In the morning's tender light,
Every hope takes wondrous flight.
New paths untraveled, yet unseen,
Mark the place where dreams convene.

Shoots of green from earth ascend,
With each start, old sorrows mend.
Blossoms bright in early spring,
Herald all the joys they bring.

Fresh endeavors call our name,
Whispered softly just the same.
In each heartbeat, visions clear,
Future days draw ever near.

Yesterday's burdens fade away,
A brand-new dawn, a brighter day.
Strength is found in every scar,
Guiding us to who we are.

New beginnings, bold and true,
Every sunrise, skies anew.
With each step, we start afresh,
Life renews in endless mesh.

As each chapter turns the page,
In our hearts, we disengage.
Finding courage, we advance,
In the rhythm of life's dance.

Healing Waters

Beneath the calm, reflective streams,
Lie the depths of whispered dreams.
Healing waters, tender, pure,
Of silent solace, they assure.

Rivers flow, serenely gliss,
In their embrace, sweet bliss.
Each ripple holds a gentle note,
Carrying hope, keeping us afloat.

Seas of azure, vast and wide,
Washing grief from the inside.
In their waves, we find release,
A silent promise, offered peace.

Moments lost to tears and rain,
Washed away, removing pain.
In these waters, spirits rise,
Bathing in their tranquil guise.

Healing waters, crystal clear,
Drawing close, emotions near.
From the depths, we surface strong,
To life again, where we belong.

Rays of Resilience

Through shadowed days and starless nights,
Rays of strength ignite our sights.
In the heart of darkest storms,
Resilience, with grace, transforms.

From ashes, rise the phoenix flame,
Whispered tales of strength acclaim.
Unyielding spirit, fierce and bright,
Guides us through the longest night.

With every fall, we rise again,
Borrowing the strength within.
Challenges, we face with might,
Turning darkness into light.

Courage flows through every vein,
Unwavering, despite the pain.
Hope is found in every glance,
In resilience, we advance.

Rays of fortitude shine clear,
Shattering the grip of fear.
From the depths, we climb anew,
In resilience, we are true.

Glistening Paths

Beneath the canopy's gentle sway,
Glistening paths in morning's light.
Dew-kissed leaves in soft array,
Whispers of dawn in vivid sight.

Songbirds chirp in melodies sweet,
A tapestry of nature's song.
Footsteps on the earthen sheet,
Life's dance where we belong.

Emerald trees encircle care,
Roots entwine in nature's weave.
Every breath, a sacred prayer,
For the freedom we receive.

Onward through the forest's arms,
Guided by the light above.
Embracing every subtle charm,
In this realm of endless love.

Sunrise through the branches gleam,
Casting shadows soft and fleet.
In this place where dreams redeem,
Nature's heart and ours meet.

Seeds of Joy

From tiny seeds in fertile ground,
Sprouts joy that rises high.
In every petal, love is found,
Reaching up to kiss the sky.

Beneath the sun's embracing glow,
Life's wonders start to bloom.
With gentle winds, the seeds will grow,
Brushing away any gloom.

Laughter dances on the breeze,
Hope is rooted deep within.
With each hug and word that frees,
Our garden thrives again.

Nurtured by both rain and light,
Tender bonds begin to form.
In the warmth of days and nights,
Hearts and nature transform.

Through the seasons, hand in hand,
We sow the seeds of pure delight.
Harvesting a joyful land,
Where every dawn brings new light.

Soulful Mornings

In the hush of dawn's embrace,
Soulful mornings gently wake.
Golden rays on nature's face,
Murmurs of the day they make.

Softly tread through dew-kissed fields,
Whispers of the earth are heard.
Every step, a heart that yields,
To the song of morning's word.

Sky adorned in pastel shades,
Brushstrokes of a painter's dream.
Curtains of the night now fade,
Light with love begins to beam.

Birds take flight in graceful arcs,
Heralds of a world reborn.
Echoes fill the quiet parks,
In the calm of soulful morn.

With each breath, a peace profound,
Moments wrapped in tranquil air.
In these mornings, love is found,
Souls commune without a care.

Unwritten Seasons

In the dance of time's long stride,
Unwritten seasons come anew.
Whispers on the changing tide,
Paint the skies in varied hues.

Leaves will fall and flowers rise,
Cycles of the earth's embrace.
Nature writes in wistful sighs,
Stories of each sacred place.

Winter's chill and summer's heat,
Mark the passage, year by year.
Moments blend, as memories meet,
Held within our hearts so dear.

Through the springtime's gentle kiss,
Autumn's gold and winter's frost.
Every turn, a fleeting bliss,
Yet no season's ever lost.

In life's book, each page we pen,
With unseen grace and silent rhyme.
Treasured whispers, now and then,
In the chapters of our time.

Heaven's Dawn

In the silence of the early light,
Angels whisper dreams anew.
Stars retreat, the dark takes flight,
A canvas painted gold and blue.

Soft breezes hum a tender song,
Blossoms wake from night's embrace.
Nature's choir sings along,
Peaceful dawn, a gift of grace.

Mountains glow with morning's kiss,
Rivers shimmer, pure and clear.
Heaven's dawn, a moment's bliss,
Bringing hope and wiping fear.

Birds in chorus greet the day,
Skies alight with wings in flight.
In the dawn, we find our way,
Guided by the morning light.

Awaited Peace

Whispered dreams in twilight's glow,
Hope ascends, dispelling strife.
In the stillness, hearts do know,
Peace awaits in quiet life.

Ripples dance on tranquil streams,
Reflecting skies of azure hue.
In the calm, we weave our dreams,
Under heaven's timeless blue.

Echoes of a distant song,
Gentle as the evening breeze.
In its cadence, we belong,
Finding solace, finding ease.

Candles flicker, shadows play,
Night enfolds in soft embrace.
In the quiet, we shall stay,
Awaited peace, our sacred place.

Shining Paths

Golden rays through canopies,
Light the paths we walk in grace.
In the forest, 'neath the trees,
Life's true beauty, we embrace.

Pebbles glisten, dew adorned,
Secrets whispered by the leaves.
On these paths, our souls reborn,
In the dance of dawn's reprieves.

Winding roads of endless light,
Beckon forth with gentle sway.
Guided by the purest sight,
Following the break of day.

Steps in sync with nature's call,
Bound by threads of fate and time.
In the glow, we stand tall,
On shining paths, our spirits climb.

Distant Lullabies

Softly sung on moonlit breeze,
Melodies of lands afar.
Gentle tunes that whisper, please,
Guide us by the evening star.

In the hush of night, we dream,
Of places where our hearts can fly.
Lulled by songs, a silver stream,
Carried through the endless sky.

Crickets' chirps, an earthly choir,
Harmony in shadows cast.
In each note, a secret fire,
Burns the memories of the past.

Waves of night in rhythmic sway,
Cradling minds to realms serene.
Distant lullabies convey,
Dreams beyond what eyes have seen.

Dawn's Embrace

Cool winds whisper through the trees
The night begins to fade away
A new light dances on the seas
Heralding the start of day

Birds sing out their early song
Their melodies both bright and true
The world feels right, where it belongs
Bathed in soft and golden hue

The flowers stretch to greet the sun
As shadows play upon the grass
Glistening with morning dew
In the moment, time seems to pass

Children's laughter starts to rise
Filling air with pure delight
The day's promise clear and wise
In the tender morning light

A hush of stillness wraps around
A world renewed, a sacred space
With every heartbeat, gentle sound
Found within the dawn's embrace

Serene Future

Clouds adrift in skies of blue
A calm horizon beckons near
Paths we follow, bright and true
Echo dreams we hold so dear

Endless fields of emerald green
Stretch out as far from here to there
A world of wonders yet unseen
Calls us to a future fair

Waves that kiss the sandy shore
Speak of timeless, gentle grace
With each breath, we long for more
In the future's sweet embrace

Stars above in vast array
Guide us through the night's tender veil
As night turns gently into day
On a serene future's trail

Hope revived within our hearts
In every dawn's embracing light
A journey's end, with fresh new starts
Into the future pure and bright

Dream's Gateway

When night descends with velvet hand
And dreams invite us to their dance
In realms untold we take a stand
Within this ethereal romance

Doors of wonder open wide
With each star a guiding flame
Across the cosmos, we glide
In dreams, we're never the same

Mystic rivers carved from light
Flow through nights of boundless grace
With a whisper, dreams take flight
Beyond time and open space

Painted skies and lavender plains
Unreal kingdoms, yet so true
In these realms, no sorrow reigns
Only magic, through and through

As dawn approaches, soft and clear
We leave the dream's enchanting sway
Yet carry its light, near and dear
Back from gateway, break of day

Waking Optimism

Morning's breath upon my face
Whispers of a brand new start
Moments wrapped in purest grace
Fill with joy a beating heart

Opportunities arise
As sunlight breaks the night's dark veil
Hope reflected in the skies
In every sunrise, a new tale

Eyes alight with future's gleam
Boundless possibilities
Life, a river and a stream
Flowing towards new destinies

Every step a choice we make
Turning dreams to lived belief
Building bridges for love's sake
Crafting futures beyond grief

With every dawn, renewed we stand
Casting shadows of old fears
In waking optimism, hand in hand
We embrace what faith endears

Dawn's Renewal

The night gives way to morning,
A canvas bathed in light.
Birds begin their calling,
Signaling the end of night.

The first rays touch the earth,
Golden hues, a tender kiss.
Awakening nature's mirth,
In this moment of pure bliss.

Miracles in each new day,
Hope reborn in sunrise's hue.
Guiding all who've lost their way,
To the dawn's bright avenue.

Whispers in the gentle breeze,
Songs of promise, fresh and true.
Nature's symphony to please,
Every heart that's feeling blue.

From shadows into brilliance bright,
The world is born once more.
In the beauty of morning light,
We find peace, forevermore.

Hope Unfurled

In the darkest hours of night,
A spark of hope is seen.
Casting out the dread and fright,
With promises serene.

From the ash of past despair,
Rises hope on wings of gold.
In the tender, gentle air,
New stories to unfold.

Each heartache left behind,
Gives space for dreams to fly.
Courage in the hopeful kind,
Illuminates the sky.

When life's trials seem unfair,
Trust in hope's enduring gleam.
In its light, find strength to bear,
And fulfill each cherished dream.

With every step you take,
Let hope be your guide.
In its light, decisions make,
And in its strength, abide.

Refreshed Spirit

In the stillness of the dawn,
A refreshed spirit wakes.
With the darkness fully gone,
New energy it takes.

Whispers of the morning air,
Cleanse the worries of the night.
Heart and soul in tandem share,
The promise of the light.

Nature's call to rise anew,
Echoes through the tranquil day.
Voices in the morning dew,
Guide us on our way.

The spirit finds its strength within,
Renewed by the dawn's first light.
Embracing all that life has been,
With love and strength in sight.

Breathe in deep the fresh, new start,
Let go of every fear.
With a refreshed, renewed heart,
Face the day, sincere.

Brighter Tomorrows

In the shadows of today,
Lies the light of future's beam.
Guiding on a hopeful way,
Towards every cherished dream.

Brighter tomorrows wait ahead,
Beyond the trials we face.
In each step where we are led,
We find strength in grace.

Promises of what will be,
Hang on the horizon's line.
In the darkness, we still see,
Glimpses of a sign.

Every dawn breaks with new hope,
For a better day to come.
Helping hearts and minds to cope,
As we together hum.

Sing the song of brighter days,
Lift your voice in cheerful chorals.
Walk in light's embracing rays,
Towards brighter tomorrows.

Chasing the Horizon

Beneath the sky so vast and free,
We chase the edge of the unseen sea,
Where dream and daylight intertwine,
And shadows dance on the horizon line.

With each step taken, closer we draw,
To realms where mystic wonders awe,
Our hearts, they pound with endless might,
In pursuit of the horizon's light.

The wind whispers secrets of the old,
Stories of ventures, brave and bold,
In the glow of twilight's tender kiss,
Our souls find solace, boundless bliss.

Mountains high and valleys low,
Craft the journey as we go,
In this race against the fading sun,
Chasing horizons till we're one.

We seek the end in every start,
With hope and dreams that never part,
Onward to horizons new,
Chasing dreams with skies so true.

Illuminated Tomorrows

Amidst the dark, a beacon's glow,
Guiding hearts through night's soft flow,
Whispers of the dawn to come,
Promise of a brighter drum.

Stars that fade, give rise to light,
Turning shadows into sight,
Tomorrow's hues in morning's blush,
Banishing the midnight hush.

Paths unknown, yet brightly lit,
With hopes and dreams we tightly knit,
In every gleam, a story borrowed,
From illuminated tomorrows.

Through trials faced and battles fought,
In light, we find the strength we've sought,
Each dawn, a canvas fresh and new,
With colors bold and spirits true.

Our past behind, the future bright,
In each step forward, pure delight,
Embrace the luminescent day,
With tomorrows that illuminate our way.

Silent Sunrises

In the hush before daybreak's glow,
When the world is still, and movements slow,
A gentle kiss of light appears,
Silent sunrise dries night's tears.

Veils of twilight drift away,
Welcoming the brand new day,
Golden rays in subtle surmise,
Whisper secrets of the skies.

Every dawn a quiet song,
Softly breaking, never wrong,
With whispered tales of hope and grace,
In morning's tender, warm embrace.

Tranquil moments, still and clear,
As the silent sun draws near,
Bids the night its soft goodbyes,
With a promise in the sunrise.

Silent sunrises paint the dawn,
With brushes dipped in pale élan,
In their quiet, gentle rise,
We find peace in new sunrise.

Ray's Prelude

Before the day reveals its face,
A prelude sung in silent grace,
The first light of the rising ray,
Heralds the coming of the day.

Shadows stretch as darkness wanes,
Illuminating forests, plains,
Whispers of the dawn's embrace,
In each ray, a warm, soft trace.

Prelude to a symphony,
Of morning light and distant sea,
As dawn breaks with gentle ease,
It carries comforting, breezy pleas.

Nature stirs in tender awe,
At the beauty without flaw,
With each ray, a tale untold,
Of warmth, and light, and stories old.

Ray's prelude, a start anew,
Casting skies in vibrant hue,
From the first light's tender kiss,
We find our morning's simple bliss.

Blooming Hopes

In a garden lush, dreams arise
Under skies of azure vast
Petals open, bid goodbyes
To the shadows of the past

Whispers soft in morning dew
Sing of days yet to unfold
In the green, a chance anew
Stories spun in threads of gold

Sunlit beams and blossoms bright
Pave the paths of bloom and cheer
Hope awakens with the light
Promises of spring draw near

Fragrant winds through branches twine
Crafting tales of silent grace
Every heart in hope align
In this timeless, sacred space

Blooming hopes, like springtime's call
Guide us through the seasons' flow
For in every rise and fall
There's a seed to plant and grow.

Faith's Horizon

Across the dawn, a beacon shines
Guiding hearts with tender gleam
Through the night, its light aligns
With the paths of every dream

In the hush, a whisper speaks
Of the strength to find our way
Faith in every heart that seeks
Hope to greet another day

Mountains high and valleys low
In the journey, faith persists
Holding fast through ebb and flow
Wisdom in its gentle mists

Every step we take in trust
Builds the bridge to skies serene
Faith that turns our fears to dust
Shapes the world in hopeful sheen

On faith's horizon, visions clear
Guide us past the stormy seas
With each dawn that draws us near
We find solace and sweet peace.

Visions Unseen

Beyond the veil, where dreams reside
Lies a realm of silent grace
In each heart, the visions hide
Traces of a timeless place

Stars that glisten, whispering
Tales of futures yet to weave
In their light, bright wonders sing
Of the gifts that we receive

Paths unseen, yet softly bright
Guide our souls through night and day
In the dark, the secret light
Shows us where our hopes may lay

Silent shores of mystery
Hold the keys to what may start
In these visions, we may see
The true compass of the heart

Through the mists of doubt and fear
Wander visions, bold and grand
In the dreamscape, oh so clear
We find hope in every hand.

Breaking Dawn

In the still of morning's hush
Rays of gold begin to break
Through the night's embracing blush
Comes a world anew, awake

Shadows flee as light appears
In the dawn, a promise made
Brush away the silent tears
With each new, bright serenade

Crimson skies and softened hues
Paint the day with hope's advance
Breaking dawn, a sacred muse
Leading hearts in joy's dance

With each ray that lights the sky
Comes a call to start again
Breaking dawn, we rise and fly
Casting off the dark of then

In the fullness of the morn
Life's renewal sings aloud
Breaking dawn, in splendor worn
Lifts our spirits, proud and proud.

Sunlit Journey

Beneath the sun's embrace, we tread,
Golden paths, where dreams are led.
Whispers of hope in the air,
Guiding hearts with tender care.

Footprints mark our quest for grace,
Each step leaves a gentle trace.
In fields of gold, where daisies bloom,
We find our joy, dispelling gloom.

Sunrise kisses dew-kissed earth,
Gifting moments full of mirth.
Hand in hand, through light we stride,
Forever strong, with love as guide.

Journeys end as sunsets flame,
Evening whispers, soft and tame.
Reflections of the day now past,
Memories built to forever last.

In twilight's glow, our spirits soar,
Awaiting dawn, to dream once more.
A cycle endless, life's pure art,
Sunlit journeys warm the heart.

Morning Promises

The dawn breaks with a golden hue,
Promises fresh as morning dew.
Birds sing tales of dreams anew,
A sky that's painted, wide and blue.

Soft light kisses sleepy eyes,
Awakening hopes beyond the skies.
Fields awake as flowers bloom,
Dispelling night's lingering gloom.

Morning whispers secrets sweet,
Winds caress with gentle beat.
Time begins its daily dance,
A world reborn in morning's trance.

Sun ascends in grand display,
Heralding a bright new day.
Voices rise in joyful cheer,
New beginnings drawing near.

Each sunrise marks a chance to start,
To heal, to love, to mend the heart.
In morning's light, our spirits rise,
Embracing life with open eyes.

New Chapters

Pages turn, a story new,
In every breath, a chance to view.
Each chapter brings a different hue,
Moments painted in life's truest blue.

Embrace the folds of time, my friend,
In each new line, a path will bend.
With ink of hope, the script shall blend,
A tale of love, to never end.

Journeys vast, horizons wide,
In written words, our truths confide.
With every choice, a step beside,
Chapters penned with hearts as guide.

Beyond the past, the future gleams,
In whispered thoughts and fleeting dreams.
New pages write our silent screams,
Transforming life with vibrant themes.

In every book, potential sings,
Of joys and sorrows life may bring.
A novel born on hope's light wings,
With every chapter, new beginnings.

Whispering Skies

Underneath the whispering skies,
Stars align as dreams arise.
Winds speak tales of ancient might,
In the soft embrace of night.

Gentle breezes hum their song,
Carrying echoes all night long.
Clouds drift slow, the heavens sigh,
Tales of yore in whispered cry.

Moonlight casts a silver glow,
On tranquil lands and seas below.
Through the night, the whispers flow,
In secret tongues, the stars bestow.

Silent night, with stories shared,
In the quiet, hearts are bared.
Cosmos weave their threads of light,
In an endless dance, so bright.

As dawn approaches, skies will fade,
The whispers cease, night's serenade.
Yet in our hearts, those whispers lie,
Echoes of dreams in the whispering sky.

Shining Moments

In the heart of night, stars gleam bright,
A tapestry of shimmering light,
Whispers of dreams dance in the sky,
Hope and wonder arise up high.

Beneath the moon's soft silver glow,
Through tranquil woods, soft breezes flow,
Moments fleeting, yet so grand,
Timeless secrets held in hand.

Memories etched in time's gentle sand,
Footprints left on a distant strand,
Echoes of laughter, love's sweet call,
Life's fleeting beauty, we recall.

In every twinkling light above,
In every tender act of love,
Shining moments woven tight,
Guiding us through darkest night.

So cherish each fleeting spark,
Though life may oft feel stark,
For in each moment, pure and true,
Lies the magic, the me and you.

Brighter Tomorrows

As dawn breaks with a golden hue,
New possibilities break through,
Yesterday's shadows fade away,
Promises of a brighter day.

Sunrise kisses the morning dew,
A canvas washed in colors new,
Whispers of hope in every ray,
Guiding us along the way.

In each heartbeat, dreams arise,
A symphony reaching to the skies,
Paths untraveled, stories untold,
A future bright, a world to mold.

Courage kindles the spirit's fire,
Lifting us ever higher,
Step by step, towards horizons wide,
With faith and love as our guide.

Beyond the clouds of gray and sorrow,
Lies the dawn of brighter tomorrows,
In unity, hand in hand we'll go,
Towards a future where dreams grow.

Ember of Change

In the stillness, a spark ignites,
Embers glowing in the night,
Change whispers on the wind's breath,
A dance between life and death.

From ashes, new beginnings rise,
Phoenix-like, to claim the skies,
Metamorphosis, a journey bold,
Transforming shadows into gold.

With every flame, old chains break,
A revolution in hearts awake,
The world reborn, anew it seems,
Woven from the thread of dreams.

Embrace the ember, fierce and true,
For change resides in all we do,
Guiding us with its fiery light,
Through darkest hours to day so bright.

From within the flames of old,
A future forged, stories unfold,
In every ember, the promise lies,
Of change as constant as the skies.

Winds of Renewal

Winds of change, whispers soft,
Carrying dreams aloft,
Through valleys deep and mountains high,
Guiding us under an open sky.

Breezes sweep the staleness clear,
Breathing life both far and near,
Renewal dances on the air,
A reminder that we tread with care.

Leaves unfurl in spring's embrace,
Nature's touch, a softening grace,
Cycles turn, as seasons blend,
In renewal, life begins again.

Through the storm, a cleansing call,
To rise anew after the fall,
In every gust, a tale untold,
Of courage found, of spirits bold.

So let the winds of change prevail,
Filling sails where hearts set sail,
Towards horizons fresh and true,
With every breath, we're born anew.

Starlit Paths

Under a canopy wide and vast,
Our footsteps echo from the past.
Guided by the moon's soft glow,
On starlit paths, together we go.

Whispers of night weave through the trees,
With every breath, a gentle breeze.
Stars above like silent guides,
On starlit paths, where love abides.

Mysteries of the heavens near,
In the stillness, none to fear.
Walk in silence, fate's decree,
On starlit paths, so wild and free.

Each step taken in twilight's grace,
Leads us to a hidden place.
Magic lingers in the night,
On starlit paths, wrapped in light.

Time stands still in these hours,
Bound by celestial powers.
Eternity in moments passed,
On starlit paths, made to last.

Unseen Rainbow

In the midst of a gentle rain,
Colors bloom, though not in vain.
An unseen rainbow arches high,
Hidden beauty in the sky.

Beneath clouds, where dreams reside,
Silent vows and hopes abide.
Invisibly, hues combine,
An unseen rainbow, so divine.

Through the mist, a quiet song,
Melodies where hearts belong.
Promises in droplets fall,
An unseen rainbow, standing tall.

Glistening through the morning dew,
Illusions bright and yet so true.
Nature's secret, softly shown,
An unseen rainbow, brightly grown.

In the spaces eyes can't see,
Lies the core of mystery.
Trust in wonders, pure and rare,
An unseen rainbow's silent prayer.

Woven Sunlight

Threads of gold in morning air,
Woven sunlight everywhere.
Nature's loom with daylight spun,
Casting warmth from dawn till done.

Fields awaken, touched by light,
Shadows flee from day's delight.
Every leaf and blade of grass,
Woven sunlight, moments pass.

Gentle beams that soothe the skin,
Healing rays that come within.
Golden tendrils in the breeze,
Woven sunlight through the trees.

Silent symphony of day,
Woven in a bright array.
Colors blend in harmony,
Woven sunlight, wild and free.

Evening comes, the threads unwind,
Leaving warmth in hearts and mind.
Grateful for the light once shown,
Woven sunlight, fully grown.

Promise of Daybreak

Night dissolves in dawning light,
Stars retreat from out of sight.
Hope ascends on morning's crest,
Promise of daybreak, gentle rest.

Through the twilight, dreams unfold,
Touched by rays of liquid gold.
Future whispers in the haze,
Promise of daybreak's early gaze.

Birdsong marks the journey's start,
Healing wounds of weary hearts.
Fears and shadows swept away,
Promise of daybreak, bright and gay.

In the stillness, silent prayer,
Life renews in morning air.
Fresh beginnings, pure and true,
Promise of daybreak, skies anew.

Each dawn brings a sacred vow,
Moments lived and here and now.
Cherish every breath we take,
Promise of daybreak, love awake.

Paths of Sunshine

In the jasmine fields where dawn begins,
Golden threads weave the light,
Footsteps whisper on a trail of dreams,
Guided softly by the white.

Meadows dance with gentle hum,
Beneath the azure, wide and grand,
Sunbeams sketch stories, unchained,
On an endless canvas of sand.

Every path holds secret beams,
Woven from the morning's smile,
A promise in each step, it seems,
To walk along the radiant mile.

Trees embrace the laughter bright,
Branches arch in graceful sway,
Pathways kissed by gentle light,
Show the sunshine's tender way.

Daylight whispers soft and warm,
In the fields where hopes begin,
Paths of sunshine slowly form,
And the world feels much akin.

Infinite Mornings

Through the mists of early dawn,
Cerulean skies unfold,
Songs of daybreak moving on,
Stories yet untold.

Mountains greet the birth of light,
Shadows fade in morn's embrace,
Infinite mornings in their flight,
Leave a tranquil trace.

Breezes hush the world awake,
With lullabies of still and peace,
Infinite mornings softly take,
All that restless nights release.

Colors merge as dawn ascends,
Soft the whispers of the breeze,
Infinite mornings like old friends,
Guard our dreams with ease.

Between the night and day's first sigh,
Magic in the air suspends,
Infinite mornings paint the sky,
With a love that never ends.

Rays of Possibility

In the silent dawn's embrace,
Glows a world of endless might,
Dreams do shimmer in their place,
In the early morning light.

Every sunrise whispers hope,
Through the calm and gentle air,
Rays of possibility grope,
For the hearts that truly dare.

Golden beams ignite the sky,
Paths to futures yet unseen,
In their warmth, our spirits fly,
Boundless are the dreams we glean.

Dewdrops catch the morning gleam,
Reflecting wishes in our gaze,
In the rays of possibilities,
We find our destinies amaze.

Every dawn a canvas new,
Brushed with endless light and grace,
In each ray a truth anew,
In each heart, a wondrous space.

Whispers of Radiance

In the hush of early day,
Bright whispers gently start,
Radiant beams begin their play,
To warm each waking heart.

Sunrise sings a soft refrain,
Echoes float on morning air,
Whispers of radiance remain,
In moments pure and rare.

Shadows flee with dawn's first touch,
Dreams lift higher day by day,
Whispers of radiance mean so much,
As night fades far away.

Glimmers waltz on morning dew,
Hints of gold in every breeze,
Whispers of radiance, songs anew,
Murmured through the trees.

Come the daybreak, soft and kind,
Radiance whispers, then takes flight,
Leaving gentle sparks behind,
To light our path with tender light.

Gleaming Horizons

Beneath the sky where dreams are spun,
The golden threads of dawn begun,
A voyage to the endless sun,
In realms where hearts and hopes are won.

The waves of time, they gently kiss,
Our footsteps traced in twilight's bliss,
In every shimmer, every gliss,
We chase horizons' boundless kiss.

Beyond the mountains, past the veil,
Where whispered dreams and hopes prevail,
A journey on the starlit trail,
To realms where every heart can sail.

The gleaming path before our eyes,
Reflecting in the endless skies,
The promise of a new sunrise,
Where every fleeting shadow dies.

From dawn to dusk, the light we chase,
In every breath, a warm embrace,
As long as hope and dreams we place,
We'll find horizons' timeless grace.

Sunrise of Hope

Awake with dawn, the world anew,
The sky ablaze with hopeful hue,
From night's embrace, the morning grew,
A chance for dreams to come in view.

The whispered winds of morning's grace,
Brush gently 'cross each sleepy face,
In every light-filled, sacred space,
The promise of a new embrace.

With every ray that warms the earth,
A song of life and love gives birth,
The morning's glow of endless worth,
A beacon shining through the dearth.

In every heartbeat, every breath,
Escaping shadows, doubt, and death,
We rise with hope, no fears to fence,
And greet the dawn with calm expense.

Align with dawn, our spirits soar,
New worlds await to be explored,
In every sunrise, dreams restore,
The promise of forevermore.

Echoes of Tomorrow

The echo of tomorrow's dream,
Whispers through the moonlit stream,
A gentle sigh, a silent scream,
In night's embrace, the stars redeem.

Across the void, where shadows sleep,
A promise made, a secret keep,
Through space and time, our souls do leap,
In rhythms where the heartbeats steep.

Tomorrow's song, a distant chime,
A melody through space and time,
In every note, a climb, a rhyme,
To dreams where hopes and futures shine.

The echoes blend, a twilight's tone,
In landscapes where the unknown's sown,
In every thought, a seed is thrown,
From which tomorrow's world is grown.

In every breath of dawn, we find,
The silent whispers left behind,
The echoes of tomorrow's mind,
A tapestry by fate designed.

Whispered Promises

In twilight's hush, the whispers breeze,
Through silent woods and rustling trees,
A promise carried on the seas,
Of endless love and memories.

The moonlight casts a silver glow,
On pathways where the dreamers go,
In shadows past, the promises flow,
Where hearts confide in undertow.

The stars above in quiet gaze,
Bear witness to the love's embrace,
In silent whispers, softly trace,
The promises that time can't erase.

Each breath, a vow in night's allure,
A secret kept, a heart's secure,
In whispered winds, the soul's demure,
With promises of love so pure.

Through night to dawn, the secrets keep,
In dreams and shadows, softly steep,
A whispered promise, ever deep,
In hearts where love's sweet whispers sleep.

Milton Keynes UK
Ingram Content Group UK Ltd.
UKHW051517010724
444807UK00016BA/29